# DARE

# TO

# DREAM

## JOANNE CARROLL

Glendale Heights, IL 60139

## Great Quotations, Inc.

Compiled by Joanne Carroll

Cover Design by Design Dynamics
Typeset Design by Julie Otlewis

Published by Great Quotations, Inc.

Library of Congress Catalog Card Number : 98-075796

**ISBN: 1-56245-362-9**

Printed in Hong Kong 2000

This book is  dedicated to all my friends who believed in me.

You know who you are.

If you can imagine it, you can achieve it. If you can dream it, you can become it.

- William Arthur Ward

When the mind of men can conceive and believe, the mind of man can achieve.

- W. Clement Stone

Your wits work when you do. In other words, act as if you had some brains. If you follow the ways of confident men, people will place you in their category.

- David Seabury

There is nothing on Earth you cannot have — once you have mentally accepted the fact  that you can have it.

- Robert Collier

Faith is to believe what you do not see; the reward for this faith is to see what you believe.

- Saint Augustine

Success is a state of mind. If you want success start thinking of yourself as a success.

- Joyce Brothers

Everyone has a talent. What is rare is the courage to follow the talent to the dark place where it leads.

- Erica Jong

Limited expectations yield only limited results.

- Susan Laurson Willig

The vision that you glorify in
your mind, the ideal that you
enthrone in your heart . . .
this you will build your life by.
This you will become.

- James Allen

You can do what you think you can do and you cannot do what you think you cannot do.

- Ben Stein

Upon deciding, be quick to act.

- Maximilien Robespierre

Every calling is great when
greatly pursued.

- Oliver Wendell Holmes

We are creators, and we can form today the world we personally shall be living in tomorrow.

- Robert Collier

You have to believe in yourself.
And you have to down deep
within the bottom of your soul,
feel that you can do the job that
you've set out to do.

- William Castle Devries

All this must start, you know,
with an idea, a mental image.

- Robert Collier

We envy those with brilliant minds and yet it sometimes seems to me we each have talents given us — our problem is to set them free.

- R. McCann

We have our brush and colors . . .
paint Paradise and in we go.

- Nikos Kazantzakis

You begin by always expecting
good things to happen.

- Tom Hopkins

Ideas are the roots of creation.

Ernest Dimnet

To think rightly is to create.

- Elbert Hubbard

To make up your mind before you start that sacrifice is part of the package.

- Richard M. Devos

The empires of the future are the empires of the mind.

- Winston Churchill

What is our praise or pride but to imagine excellence, and try to make it?

- Richard Wilbur

There is nothing either good or
bad but thinking makes it so.

- William Shakespeare

I was successful because you
believed in me.

- Ulysses S. Grant

There is no future in any job.
The future lies in the man who
holds the job.

- George Crane

The things you want are already
around you, no matter how bare
everything may look.

- Robert Collier

Keep away from people who try
to belittle your ambitions. Small
people always do that, but the
really great make you feel that
you, too, can become great.

- Mark Twain

Success or failure is often
determined on the drawing board.

- Robert J. McKain

Are you in earnest? Seize this very minute. What you can do or think you can do . . . Begin it!

- Goethe

Beware of your expectations for they have become your reality.

- Elita Darby

Doubt indulged soon becomes doubt realized.

- Francis Ridley Havergal

The best is yet to be.

- Robert Browning

There is only one quality more important than "know how." This is "know what" by which we determine not only how to accomplish our purposes but what our purposes are to be.

- Norbert  Wiener

Any idea seriously entertained
tends to bring about the
realization of itself.

- Joseph Chilton Pearce

Success is focusing the full power of all you are on what you have a burning desire to achieve.

- Wilfred A. Peterson

In the moment that you carry this conviction... in that moment your dream will become a reality.

- Robert Collier

Within our dreams and aspirations
we find our opportunities.

- Sue Atchley Ebaugh

Inner life can affect
outward events.

- Stephen Spender

Everything is possible for him
who believes.

- Mark 9:23

Each of us has within us a life force, a spirit, a principle, an essence, an unfulfilled potential, that gives no rest, no peace until it is realized.

- Peter Nivio Zarlenga

The universe is transformation;
our life is what our thoughts
make it.

- Marcus Aurelius Antonius

The wisdom of all ages and cultures emphasizes the tremendous power our thoughts have over our character and circumstances.

- Liane Cordes

The principle of life is that life responds by corresponding; your life becomes the thing you have decided it shall be.

- Raymond Charles Barker

The trouble with most people is
that they think with their hopes
or fears or wishes rather than
with their minds.

- Will Durant

Every person is the creation of himself, the image of his own thinking and believing.

- Claude M. Bristol

You have a remarkable ability which you never acknowledged before. It is to look at a situation and know whether you can do it. And I mean really know the answer.

- Carl Frederick

Saying yes means getting up and acting on your belief that you can create meaning and purpose in whatever life hands you.

- Susan Jeffers, Ph.D.

There can be no reality to the things you want until they have structure within your mind first.

- Anthony Norvell

If today your abilities are small
and your powers insignificant,
begin now to make a more
thorough use of them and they
will grow.

- Raymond Holliwell

Even a small idea of substance
may be added to and increased.

- Charles Fillmore

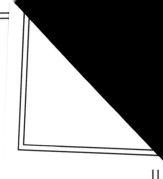

Take time to deliberate; but when the time for action arrives, stop thinking and go in.

- Andrew Jackson

A man's own self is his friend,
a man's own self is his foe.

- Bhagavad-gita

The only thing that stands between a man and what he wants from life is often merely the will to try it and the faith to believe it is possible.

- Richard M. Devos

Every outlook, desirable or
undesirable, remains possible for
anyone, no matter what his
present outlook is.

- Dr. George Weinberg

I found that I could find the
energy . . . that I could find the
determination to keep on going. I
learned that your mind can
amaze your body, if you just keep
telling yourself, I can do it . . .
I can do it!

- John Erickson

It is only by labour that thought can be made healthy, and only by thought that labour can be made happy, and the two cannot be separated with impunity.

- John Ruskin

To reach a port,
we must sail - sail,
not tie at anchor - sail, not drift.

- Franklin Delano Roosevelt

Thoughts held in mind produce
after their kind . . .

Because of the law of gravitation
the apple falls to the ground.
Because of the law of growth the
acorn becomes a mighty oak.
Because of the law of causation a
man is "as he thinketh in
his heart."

- Don Carlos Musser

Thoughts are forces ...
they have form, quality,
substance and power.

- Ralph Waldo Trine

Nothing splendid had ever been achieved except by those who dared believe that something inside of them was superior to circumstance.

- Bruce Barton

Life does not consist mainly or
even largely of the facts and
happenings. It consists mainly
of the storm of thoughts that is
forever blowing through
ones head.

- Mark Twain

In order to succeed we must first
believe that we can.

- Michael Korda

Here's the key of success and the key to failure: We become what we think about . . .

- Earl Nightingale

The stuff of the world is mind stuff.

- Sir Arthur Eddington

The only limit to our realization
of tomorrow will be our doubts
of today.

- Franklin D. Roosevelt

Nothing is easier than self deceit.
For what each man wishes, that
he also believes to be true.

- Demosthenes

Whether you think you can or think you can't . . . you are right.

- Henry Ford

Our ordinary mind always tries to persuade us that we are nothing but acorns and that our greatest happiness will be to become bigger, fatter, shinier acorns; but that is of interest only to pigs. Our faith gives knowledge of something much better: that we can become oak trees.

- E.F. Schumacher

Everything in the material universe about us, everything the universe has ever known, had its origin in thought.

- Ralph Waldo Trine

It is impossible to win the race unless you venture to run, impossible to win the victory unless you dare to battle.

- Richard M. Devos

Just one great idea can completely revolutionize your life.

- Earl Nightingale

To live is not merely to breathe, it is to act; it is to make use of our organs, senses, faculties, all of those parts of ourselves which give us the feeling of existence.

- Jean-Jacques Rousseau

What I do is prepare myself
until I know I can do what
I have to do.

- Joe Namath

I realize a long time ago that a belief which does not spring from a conviction in the emotions is no belief at all.

- Evelyn Scott

As he thinketh in his heart,
so is he.

- Proverb 28:7

No vision and you perish; no ideal, and you're lost; Your heart must ever cherish some faith at any cost. Some hope, some dream to cling to, Some rainbow in the sky, Some melody to sing to, Some service that is high.

- Harriet du Autermont

The way in which we think of ourselves has everything to do with how our world sees us and how we can see ourselves successfully acknowledged by that world.

- Arlene Raven

You can't harvest success unless
you plant the seed of success.

- Nelson Boswell

Follow your bliss.

- Joseph Campbell

They can, because they think
they can.

- Virgil

What you believe yourself to be,
you are.

- Claude M. Bristol

You determine the level of your own prosperity and achievement. You create your own circumstances.

- Donald Curtis

There is a deep tendency in human nature to become precisely what we imagine or picture ourselves to be.

- Norman Vincent Peale

Man can only be what he sees
himself to be, and only attain
what he sees himself attaining.

- Florence Scovel Shinn

The thought, the dream, the vision, always precedes the act.

- Orison Swett Marden

The strongest single factor in prosperity consciousness is self esteem; believing you can do it, believing you deserve it, believing you will get it.

- Jerry Gillies

We are what we think. All that we are arises with our thoughts. With our thoughts we make the world.

- Gautama Buddha

Think of yourself as on the threshold of unparalleled success. A whole clear glorious life before you.
Achieve! Achieve!

- Andrew Carnegie

A man consists of the faith that is in him. Whatever his faith is, he is.

- The Bhagavad-Gita

# Other Titles by Great Quotations, Inc

## Hard Covers

African American Excellence

Ancient Echoes

Attitudes of Success

Behold the Golfer

Celebrating Friendship

Commanders In Chief

Dare to Dream

First Ladies

Graduation

Golf

Good Lies for Ladies

Heartfelt Affection

Improving With Age

Inspirations for Success

Inspired Thoughts

I Thought of You Today

Journey to Success

Just Between Friends

Keys to Achieving Your Goals

Lasting Impressions

My Dear Mom

My Husband, My Love

Never Ever Give Up

Peace Be With You

Seeds of Inspiration

Seeds of Knowledge

Sharing Our Love

Sharing the Season

Smile Now

Teddy Bears

The Essence of Music

The Passion of Chocolate

The Perfect Brew

The Power of Inspiration

There's No Place Like Home

The Spirit of Christmas

Thoughts From Great Women

Great Quotations, Inc.
1967 Quincy Court
Glendale Heights, IL 60139 USA
Phone: 630-582-2800  Fax: 630-582-2813
http://www. greatquotations.com

# Other Titles by Great Quotations, Inc

## Paperbacks

A Servant's Heart
A Teacher is Better Than Two Books
I'm Not Over the Hill
Life's Lessons
Looking for Mr. Right
Midwest Wisdom
Mommy & Me
Mother, I Love You
Motivating Quotes
Mrs. Murphy's Laws
Mrs. Webster's Dictionary
Only A Sister
Parenting 101
Pink Power
Romantic Rhapsody
Social Disgraces
Stress or Sanity
The Mother Load
The Other Species
The Secret Langauge of Men
The Secret Langauge of Women
The Secrets in Your Name
Teenage of Insanity
Touch of Friendship
Wedding Wonders
Words From the Coach

## Perpetual Calendars

365 Reasons to Eat Chocolate
All Star Quotes
Always Remember Who Loves You
A Touch of Kindness
Coffee Breaks
Extraordinary Leaders
Generations
I'm a Little Stressed
I Think My Teacher Sleeps at School
Kid Stuff
My Friend & Me
Never Never Give Up
Older Than Dirt
Secrets of a Successful Mom
Shopoholic
Sweet Dreams
Teacher Zone
Tee Times
The Dog Ate My Car Keys
The Essence of Great Women
The Heart That Loves
The Honey Jar
Winning Words